RECENT ADVANCES IN CHALCONE CHEMISTRY

P. A. VIVEKANAND | P. KAMARAJ

XpressPublishing
An imprint of Notion Press

XpressPublishing
An imprint of Notion Press

No.8, 3rd Cross Street,CIT Colony,
Mylapore, Chennai, Tamil Nadu-600004

ISBN 978-1-64899-851-5

Contents

About The Authors

Dr. P. A. Vivekanand received his Doctoral degree from University of Madras and did his postdoctoral research at the prestigious Hung khuang University, Taichung, Taiwan. He has published his research findings in High Impact International Journals. Dr. P. A. Vivekanand is currently a Professor and Senior Researcher at Saveetha Engineering College(Anna University),Chennai, India.

Professor Vivekanand has taught Organo-Physical Chemistry for many years to B.S., M.S., and Ph.D students for many years. His teaching skills are exceptionally strong and these are proved by several thousand students and peer evaluations. He has presided over dozen National and International Conferences. He is acting as Editor, Reviewer and Editorial Board member of various peer reviewed international journals.

Dr. P. Kamaraj is currently the Dean [Science and Humanities] at Bharath Institute of Higher Education and Research, Chennai, India. He received his Doctoral degree from Anna University and Post Graduate degree from University of Madras. He has guided Ph.D., M.S and M.Phil students under different universities.

Professor Kamaraj has got 4 Patents and has published several research papers in high impact journals. He has authored over 6 text and reference books. His books have been prescribed as text and reference books in many Indian Universities including Anna University. He received academic and research awards including Research award from Institution of Engineers (I). He has been serving International Journals as Chief Editor, Editor and Reviewer.

- Publishers

Preface

The first aldol condensation product, 1,3-diaryl-2-propen-1-one was reported and named by Kostanecki as "Chalcones" . Chalcones are naturally occurring compounds found in various plant species like Angelica, Glycyrrhiza, Humulus and Scutellaria. Chalcones exhibit a broad spectrum of biological activities due to their small structures and Michael acceptor features, which make them tolerant to different biological molecules and enable them to readily bind.

Chemically chalcones are synthesized by two reactions namely Aldol condensation and Claisen Schmidt condensation. Chalcones are mostly synthesized by using base catalysed Claisen-Schmidt condensation reaction between equimolar quantities of aldehyde and ketone.

Due to the interesting features of the Chalcones and their most important role in medicine, the authors have made an attempt to present the current developments in the synthetic methods, biological activities and applications.

Dr. P. A.Vivekanand and Dr.P.Kamaraj

Date: 27.05.2020

Acknowledgements

Authors, Dr. P. A. Vivekanand and Dr. P. Kamaraj acknowledge the support and encouragement they received from the following authorities :

Dr. N. M. Veeraiyan - Founder President, Saveetha Engineering College, Chennai, India

Dr. S. Jagathrakshakan - Chairman, Bharath Institute of Higher Education and Research, Chennai, India.

Dr. J. Sundeep Anand - President, Bharath Institute of Higher Education and Research,Chennai, India.

Dr. Rajesh Sengodan - Director,Saveetha Engineering College, Chennai, India.

Dr. R. M. Suresh - Pro Vice Chancellor (Academics) Bharath Institute of Higher Education and Research, Chennai, India.

Dr. R. Ramesh - Principal, Saveetha Engineering College, Chennai, India

Dr. R. Hari Prakash - Additional Registrar, Bharath Institute of Higher Education and Research, Chennai, India.

Dr. S. Praveenkumar - Professor (Head - Micro Nano Design and Fabrication Centre), Saveetha Engineering College, Chennai, India

Other authorities at Saveetha Engineering College and Bharath Institute of Higher Education and Research, Chennai, India.

CHAPTER ONE

Introduction

Chalcones are 1, 3-diaryl-2-propen-1-ones in which two aromatic rings are connected by a three carbon bridge having a keto carbonyl moiety and α, β unsaturation. The chemistry of chalcones has generated exhaustive scientific studies all over the world. In particular interest has been focused on the synthesis and biodynamic activities of chalcones. The name "Chalcones" was given by Kostanecki and Tambor[1].They are aromatic ketone and an enone that forms the central core for a variety of important biological compounds, which are known collectively as chalcones or chalconoids. Privileged structures of Chalcones are structural analogues of benzalacetophenone (BAP). They are plentiful in edible plants and are considered to be precursors of flavonoids and isoflavonoids. Literature survey reveals that compounds with a chalcone-based structure have anti-inflammatory [2], anti-bacterial [3], anti-fungal [4-5], and anti-tumor activities [6-7]. These properties are largely ascribed due to the, β-unsaturated ketone moiety. Introduction of various substituents into the two aryl rings is also generating interest because it leads to useful structure-activity relationship (SAR).

In chalcones, two aromatic rings are attached by a three carbon α, β-saturated carbonyl group. Chalconoids is a very good synthon so that variety of novel heterocycles with good pharmaceutical profile can be planned. They are unsaturated ketones containing the reactive ketoethylenic group -CO-CH=CH-. These are coloured compounds because of the presence of the chromophores -CO-CH=CH-, which depend on the presence of other auxochromes. Chalconoids are characterized by the possession of a structure in which two aromatic rings A and B are linked by an aliphatic three carbon chain.

The alternative names given to chalcones are phenyl styryl ketones, beanzalacetophenone, β-phenyl acrylphenone, γ-oxo-α-γ-diphenyl-α-propylene and α- phenyl-β-benzoethylene.Generally, Chalcones are synthesized by Claisen-Schmidt condensation of aromatic aldehyde and aromatic acetophenone as ketone is either catalyzed by base or acid. Chalconoids are intermediates for synthesizing various heterocyclic compounds. Cyclization of chalcones leads to pyrimidines, pyrazline, thiazines. Chalcone and its derivatives have attracted increasing attention due to their numerous pharmacological activities. The presence of a reactive and unsaturated keto moiety as well as aryl conjugation in chalcones is found to be responsible for their biological activity.It has been demonstrated that some chalcone substituted on the aryl rings possess cytotoxic and antimitotic activity due to their ability to inhibit tubulin polymerization.They exert such effect by binding to the colchi-site of tubulin in a reversible manner.

Notwithstanding the interesting pharmacological properties demonstrated by this class of compounds, there are no chalcones as antitubulinic agents reported in clinical or pre-clinical studies. This could be attributed to their metabolic instability in vivo. In fact, the phenolic group can easily undergo phase II metabolism and the enone system can undergo Michael addition with biological nucleophiles such as glutathione. Disadvantages include: (1) chalcones are promiscuous structures with a plethora of biological activities and (2) they can have patentability problems. Hence, chalcones have been used as starting points to design and synthesize novel stable analogues with the same antimitotic effect and a better efficacy. Specifically, modifications on the chalcone scaffold regarding the replacement of the double bond have been fulfilled maintaining cytotoxicity and antitubulin action, suggesting that the double bond is not strictly required for this biological activity[8-9].

These are rich in edible plants and are considered to be precursors of flavonoids and isoflavonoids(Fig.1. and Fig.2.). Chalcones has conjugated double bonds and a completely delocalized Π-electron system on both benzene rings. Due to this, the molecules possessing such a system have relatively low redox potentials and have a greater probability of undergoing electron transfer reactions[10].

Fig. 1: Capcarthamus tinctoriustion(*Natural Source of Chalcones*)

Fig. 2 : Butterfly pea (Clitoria ternatea) flower(Natural Source of Chalcones)

Chalcone derivatives have received growing attention owing to their abundant pharmacological activities. The presence of a reactive and unsaturated keto moiety as well as aryl conjugation in chalcones is found to be responsible for their biological activities.

The treatment of bacterial infections remains a challenging therapeutic problem because of emerging infectious diseases and the increasing number of multidrug-resistant microbial pathogens. Notwithstanding many antibiotic and chemotherapeutics are available, the emergence of old and new antibiotic-resistant bacterial strains in the last decades constitutes a substantial need for new classes of anti-bacterial agents. Chalcones are α, β-unsaturated ketones and they are widespread in the plant kingdom. Generally, the majority of natural or synthetic chalcones are highly biologically active with great pharmaceutical and medicinal relevance. Furhter, chalcones are very important compounds as a Michael acceptor in organic syntheses. The Michael addition reaction is one of the most fundamental C-C bond-forming reactions in the synthesis of 1,5-dicarbonyl compounds. 1,5-Diketones are extremely important synthetic intermediates and are attractive starting materials for generating many heterocyclic [11-12] and polyfunctional compounds[13-14].

References

1. Cheng, J.H.; Hung, C.F.; *Yang, S.C.*; Wang, J.P.; Won, S.J.; Lin, C.N. Bioorg, *Med. Chem.* 2008,16,7270.

2. Avila, H.P.; Smania, E.F.; Monache, *F.D.; Smania, A.,* Bioorg. *Med. Chem.* 2008,16,9790.

3. Sortino, M.; *Delgado, P.*; Juarez, S.; *Quiroga, J.*; Abonia, R.; Insuasty, B.; Nogueras, M.; Rodero, L.; Garibotto, F.M.; Enriz, R.D.; Zacchino, S.A. Bioorg. *Med. Chem.* 2007, 15,484.

4. Vargas, M.L.Y.; Castelli, M.V.; *Kouznetsov,* V.V.; Urbina, G.J.M.; Lopez, S. N.; Sortino, M.; Enriz, R.D.; Ribas, *J.C.; Zacchino,* s. Bioorg. Med. Chem. 2003,11,1531.

5. Lopez, S.N.; Castelli, M.V.; Zacchino, S.A.; *Dominguez,* J.N.; Lobo, G.; Charris-Charris, J.; Cortes, J.C.; Ribas, J.C.; Devia, C; Rodriguez, A.M.; Enriz, R.D. Bioorg.*Med. Chem.* 2001, 8, 1999.

6. Katsori, A.M.; *Hadjipzvlou-Litina,* D. Curr. *Med. Chem.*2009, 16, 1062.

7. Achanta, G.; Modzelewska, A.; Feng,L.; Khan, S.R.; Huang, P. Mol. *Pharmacol.* 2006, 7, 426.

8. Ducki, S. Anti-cancer Agents *Med. Chem.* 2009, 9, 336.

9. Flynn, B. L.; Hamel, H.; Jung, M. K. J. *Med. Chem.* 2002, 45, 2670

10. Morrison and Boyd, Organic Chemistry, sixth edition, 2004, 971.

11. Z. S. Arigan, H. Suschitiky, *J. Chem. Soc.*, 2242 (1961).

12. F. Krohnke, Synthesis, 1, (1976).

13. E. C. Constable, A. M. W. Cargill, *J. Chem. Soc. Dalton Trans.*, 2947(1992)

14. I. R. Butler, S. J. Mcdonald, *Polyhedron*, 14,(1995) 529 .

CHAPTER TWO

Classification of Chalcones

"The good thing about science is that it's true whether or not you believe in it."

– Neil deGrasse Tyson

Chalcones are structurally one of most diverse group of flavonoids and easily allow to cyclize forming flavonoid structure which is an isomeric key step for the skeletal modifcation of chalcones. The chemistry of chalcones is still an attraction among the organic chemists from ancient days, due to the open-chain model and the feature of skeletal modification to produce a new class of organic compounds. Based on the source of generation, they are classified into two types *viz.,*Natural chalcones and Synthetic Chalcones.

2.1.Natural Chalcones

Throughout the ages, human community is reliant on nature, particularly on plants as source of carbohydrates, proteins and fats for food and shelter. In addition, plants are a valuable source of a wide range of secondary metabolites, which are used as pharmaceuticals, agrochemicals, flavours, fragrances, colours, bio pesticides and food additives. With the presence of a wide variety of secondary metabolites, plants have formed the basis for the traditional medicine systems that have been in existence for thousands of years in many countries. The flavonoids, allied phenolic and poly phenolic compounds, including tannins and derived poly-phenols and their different derivatives form one major group of phytochemicals. It has been found that in many plants flavonoids protect them against their pathogenic bacteria and fungi. The *Homo sapience* is the prime beneficiary of the dietary flavonoids knowingly or unknowingly utilizing them for prevention of diseases or cure. Their antioxidant properties, cytostatic effects in tumorigenesis and ability to inhibit a broad spectrum of enzymes have led researchers to regard these compounds as potential anticarcinogens and cardio protective agents have led researchers to regard these compounds as potential anticarcinogens and cardio protective agents.

The basic flavonoid structure is the flavan nucleus, which consists of fifteen carbon atoms arranged in three rings (C_6-C_3-C_6), which are labelled as A, B, and C. The various classes of flavonoids differ in the level of oxidation and pattern of substitution of the C ring, while individual compounds within a class differ in the pattern of substitution of the A and B rings. Chalcones (1,3-diphenyl-2-propen- 1-one, 2) are the biogenetic precursor of flavonoids abundant in edible plants in different chemical forms. Chalcone based compounds both natural and synthetic are very versatile as physiologically active compounds with a diverse array of biological activities associated with them.

Fig .1: Angelica Plant(Natural Source of Chalcones)

Fig 2: Glycyrrhiza Plant(Natural Source of Chalcones)

The therapeutic potential of the chalcone based compounds is supported by their ease of preparation, potential of oral administration, safety and profound natural abundance(Fig.1-4). In the last decade, the devotion of tremendous effort around the world to elucidate the mechanisms of these chalconoids for their unparallel array of biological activities was witnessed. Consequently, a number of synthetic methods have also been developed for the synthesis of this very important class of molecules including the structural modification of the core chalcone moiety. Chemically, chalcones are open chain flavonoids where two aromatic rings are joined by three carbon α,β unsaturated carbonyl system. Variation in the use of the core chalcone moiety is mainly based on traditional medicine for different ailments have been reported to contain a substantial amount of these chalconoids[10-11].

Chalcones are important constituents of many natural products. They are abundant in edible plants where they are considered to be the precursors of flavonoids and isoflavonoids. There is a growing interest in the pharmacological potential of chalcones which constitutes an important group of natural and synthetic products that have been screened for a wide range of pharmacological activities such as antibacterial, antitumor, anti-inflammatory, antifungal and antioxidant properties.

Fig .3: Humulus Plant(Natural Source of Chalcones)

Fig. 4 : Scutellaria Plant(Natural Source of Chalcones)

Chalcones are also well known intermediates for synthesizing various heterocyclic compounds. Several methods have been reported for the synthesis of chalcones, among which aldol condensation and Claisen-Schmidt condensation between aryl ketones and aromatic aldehydes in acidic or basic media still occupy prominent positions. Chalcones are characterized by possessing an enone moiety between two aromatic rings.

Elemental sulfur has been well known to act as an antifungal agent for a long time. Several naturally occurring antifungal agents are also known to contain sulfur.

Chalcone (1,3-diphenyl-2-propen-1-one) is a phenolic compound which is abundant in vegetables. Naturally occurring chalcones as well as synthetic chalcone analogues have demonstrated many pharmaceutical effects, including anti-inflammatory, anti-oxidant, anti-parasite, and anti-tumor activities [3-9]. Recent studies revealed that chalcones (chalcone and synthetic chalcone analogues) can inhibit NO synthesis and inducible NO synthetase (iNOS) and cycloxygenase 2 (COX-2) protein expression in lipopolysaccharide (LPS)-stimulated cells, and indicated the importance of chalcones as anti-inflammatory agents [10]. However, current knowledge regarding the anti-inflammatory effects of chalcones in vertebrates has all been reported in vitro. Thus, it is essential to establish an effective animal model to study the in vivo the anti-inflammatory effects of chalcones.

Inflammation is a complex biological event of a tissue response to a harmful stimulus (bacterial infection, burn or wound, for example). Acute inflammation usually involves dynamic regulation of pro-inflammatory mediators (Mpx, NFκB, TNFα) and the recruitment of white blood cells to harmed sites [11]. Neutrophils are one type of white blood cells which can migrate towards the harmed sites and are considered as the hallmark of acute inflammation [9]. For this reason, monitoring the number and the migration activity of neutrophils is an efficient way to evaluate acute inflammatory responses.

The optical transparency of zebrafish embryos allows non invasive and dynamic imaging of the inflammation process *in vivo*. Especially, a transgenic zebrafish line Tg (mpx:gfp) expressing green fluorescent protein (GFP) under the control of neutrophil-specific mpx promoter enables us to count the number and to monitor the migration activity of neutrophils more efficiently [1]. In this study, a wounded zebra fishmodel was used to assess the anti-inflammatory effects of chalcones (chalcone and chalcone analogues) on wound-induced inflammation *in vivo*. Also the Mpx expression was evaluated by histochemical staining, and the protein levels of three evolutionarily conserved pro-inflammatory factors (Mpx, NFκB, and TNFα) were examined upon chalcones treatment.

2.2. Synthetic chalcones

Generally Chalconoids are prepared by condensation reactions *via* base or acid catalysis. While chalcones are one type of easily synthesizable α,β-unsaturated ketone, new techniques and procedures have recently been reported due to their interesting biological activities and the development of various catalysts or reaction conditions.

Synthesis of some novel halogen substituted chalcone analogues with 5-chlorothiophene moiety using the conventional base-catalyzed Claisen-Schmidt condensation, their crystal structures and the evaluation of their antimicrobial, ferric ion and cupric ion reducing power abilities have been reported[12-13].

Numerous methods have been reported for the synthesis of 2'-hydroxychalcones and flavanones. Nevertheless, these methods are associated with several drawbacks such as poor yield, long reaction time and involvement of expensive catalysts. Besides, flavanones are always synthesized in two steps; in the first step, 2'-hydroxychalcones are prepared *via* the most commonly used method, Claisen-Schmidt condensation reaction between 2-hydroxyacetophenones and benzaldehydes in the presence of aqueous alkaline bases. Second step involves subsequent cyclization of 2'- hydroxychalcones intermediate to form flavanones. Nevertheless, conversion of chalcones into flavanones completes and gives mixture of products. Also, during 2'- hydroxychalcones synthesis, either the reaction never completes to give 2'-hydroxychalcones in high yield or part of 2'-hydroxychalcones cyclised to flavanone and give a mixture of chalocone and flavanone leading to tedious and time consuming column chromatographic separations. In spite of several drawbacks associated with chalcones and flavanones synthetic methods, to date, there is no previous report which describes the flavanones synthesis in one step. Moreover, in the last two decades, use of microwave energy for conducting organic reactions has become a very popular and emerging technique as it has several advantages over classical organic reactions such as shortening reaction times, improving yields and promoting environmental friendly (Green chemistry) new reactions.

References

1. Rao, S. R.; Ravishankar, G. A. Biotecnol. Adv.2002, 20, 101.
2. Cowan, M. M. Clin. Microbiol.Rev. 1999, 20, 564.
3. Go, M. L., Wu, X., & Liu, X. L. (2005). Chalcones: an update on cytotoxic and chemoprotective properties. Current Medicinal Chemistry, 12(4), 483.

4. 4.Awasthi S. K., Mishra N., Kumar B., Sharma M., Bhattacharya A., Mishra L. C. &Bhasin V. K. (2009). Potent antimalarial activity of newly synthesized substituted chalconeanalogsin vitro.Medicinal Chemistry Research, 18(6), 407.

5. Aponte J. C., Verástegui M., Málaga E., Zimic M., Quiliano M., Vaisberg A. J., & Hammond G. B. (2008). Synthesis, cytotoxicity, and anti-Trypanosomacruzi activity of new chalcones.Journal of Medicinal Chemistry, 51(19), 6230.

6. Alam M. S. (2012). Biological Potentials of Chalcones A Review.International Journal of Pharmaceutical & Biological Archive, 3(6).

7. Nasir Abbas Bukhari S., Jasamai M., Jantan I., & Ahmad W. (2013).Review of methods and various catalysts used for chalcone synthesis, Mini-Reviews in Organic Chemistry, 10(1), 73.

8. Ducki, S. Anti-cancer Agents Med. Chem. 2009, 9, 336.

9. Romagnoli, R.; Baraldi, P. G.; Carrion, M. D.; Cara, C. L.; Cruz-Lopez, O.; Preti, D.; Tolomeo, M.; Grimaudo, S.; Di Cristina, A.; Zonta, N.; Balzarini, J.; Brancale, A.;Sarkar, T.; Hamel, E. Bioorg.Med. Chem. 2008, 16, 5367.

10. Morrison and Boyd, Organic Chemistry, sixth edition, 2004, 971.

11. Alam M. S. (2012). Biological Potentials of Chalcones A Review.International Journal of Pharmaceutical & Biological Archive, 3(6).

12. Alcaraz, L.E.; Blanco, S.E.; Puig, O.N.; Tomas, F.; Ferretti, F.H. Antibacterial activity of flavonoids against methicillin-resistant Staphylococcus aureusstrains. J. Theor. Biol. 2000, 205, 231.

13. Echeverria, C.; Santibañez, J.F.; Donoso-Tauda, O.; Escobar, C.A.; Ramirez-Tagle, R. Structural antitumoral activity relationships of synthetic chalcones. Int. J. Mol. Sci. 2009, 10, 221.

CHAPTER THREE

Synthesis of Chalcones

"Research is to see what everybody else has seen, and to think what nobody else has thought."

—

Albert Szent-Györgyi

Privileged structures of Chalcones have a modest privileged scaffold found in many naturally occurring compounds. These structures have been usually used as a template in medicinal chemistry which facilitates a variety of substitutions with the easy synthesis for the drug discovery. Commonly, synthesis of chalcones was achieved through condensation reactions by using acid or base catalysis. Now a days, various synthetic methods and procedures have been reported due to their remarkable biological applications. The prominent synthetic strategies for the synthesis of chalcones are listed below:

- Claisen–Schmidt Condensation.
- Suzuki Coupling.
- Heck Reaction
- Wittig Reaction.
- Friedel–Crafts Acylation with Cinnamoyl Chloride

Generally, Chalconoids and its derivatives are synthesized using Claisen-Schmidt reaction, by reacting acetophenone or its derivative with benzaldehyde or its derivative in the presence of a strong base, such as KOH, NaOH, or NaH in a polar solvent (**Scheme 1**). Other catalysts such as sodium phosphate doped sodium nitrite and aluminum-magnesium hydroxide hydrate are also used .

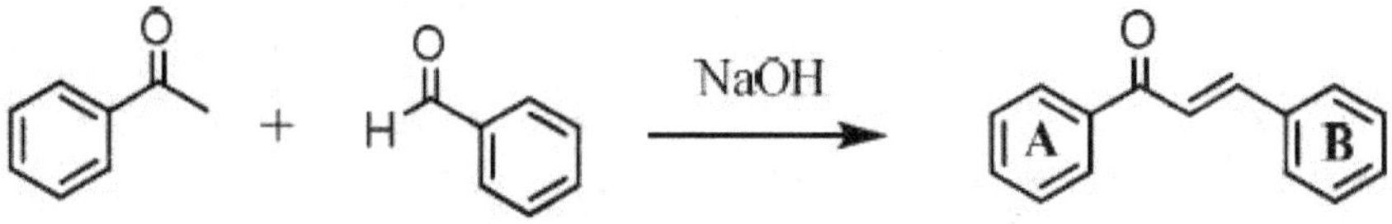

Scheme 1: General representation ofClaisen-Schmidt reaction

Solid phase Claisen-Schmidt reaction utilizing various solid catalysts was applied to synthesize chalcones by different scientific group. In this reaction, Chloro bounded resin was treated with derivatives of benzaldehydes using NaOH as catalyst(**Scheme 2**). Cross aldol condensation catalyzed by complex of Co(II)-pyridine polymer was applied to synthesize chalconoids. The complex of Co(II)-cross linking 4-vinyl pyridine-styrene showed the finest results, in which no side product was observed. Solid phase synthesis of chalcones using 2-chlorotrytilchloride as supporting resin has also been performed. Intially, the hydroxy-acetophenone derivatives was formed in methanol. The formed hydroxychalcones were then released by the addition of trichloro acetic acid [4,5].

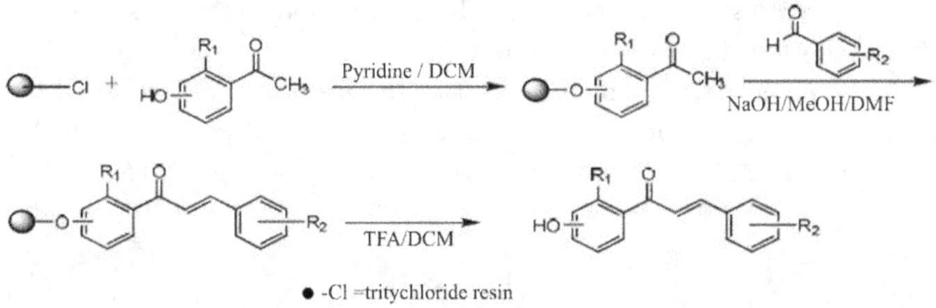

Scheme 2: General representation ofSolid phaseClaisen-Schmidt reaction

In the synthesis of chalcone, good yield are expected in solid phase cross aldol condensation employing magnesium hydrogen sulphate and self condensation products were not observed. Applying the principles of green chemistry, solvent free Claisen-Schmidt reaction was conducted using a polymer as supporting material and TBD (1,5,7-trisazabicyclo[4,4,0]dec-en) as catalyst . Further, solid phase synthesis of chalcones was also conducted using silica-sulfuric acid as catalyst(Scheme 3)[6-8]

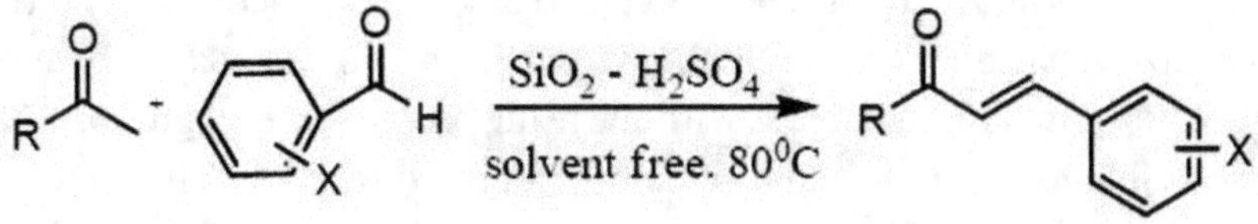

R = 4-biphenyl (or) 9H-2-fluorenyl

Scheme 3: Solid phaseClaisen-Schmidt reaction in presence of silica-sulfuric acid as catalyst

Practising an environmentally benign reaction by employing Zn (L-proline)2 as catalyst in the synthesis of chromonyl-chalcones in water resulted in Chalcone. The importance of this protocol was the use of water as solvent which is nontoxic, cheap, and non-flammable. Furthermore, Zn (L-proline) can be easily recovered and reused several times without major loss of its performing abilities [9].

Microwave irradiation induced reaction in the chalcones synthesis is one more option to synthesize chalcones. In this reaction method, the reaction time is shortened and the purification procedure is simplified(Scheme 4). Cross aldol condensation by means of microwave irradiation was used for the synthesis of chalcone analogue *viz.*, 2,6-bis(benzyliden)-cyclohexanone employing BMPTO (bis-(4-methoxyphenyl)-telluroxide) as catalyst [10].

Scheme 4: Microwave protocol in the synthesis of 2,6-bis(benzyliden)-cyclohexanone in presence of BMPTO (bis-(4-methoxyphenyl)-telluroxide) as catalyst

Smart single step synthesis protocol of chalcone was reported, in which chalcones were synthesized using molecular iodine impregnated over neutral alumina as catalyst, and employing microwave irradiation as source of energy without any solvent [11]. Using this reaction condition, polyhydroxychalcones are prepared by reacting hydroxylatedacetophenone and hydroxylatedbenzaldehyde without using any protecting group, which is impossible to be conducted by alkaline catalyzed reaction. The molecular iodine acts as Lewis acid, which facilitates the enolisation of the hydroxyl aryl ketone as well as activates the carbonyl group of hydroxyl benzaldehyde towards nucleophilic attack. The neutral alumina powder aids in enlarging the effective catalytic surface area(Scheme 5).

$$I_2 - Al_2O_3, MW$$

Scheme 5: Microwave protocol in the synthesis of Chalcone in presence of neutral alumina

Jayapal et.al., reported acid catalysed synthesis of hydroxylatedchalcones without any protecting step. The acid catalyst was prepared in situ from Thionyl chloride and ethanol [12]. The amalgamation of continuous flow processes and microwave technology technique offers many advantages, both in technical and economical aspects. Employing this technique, synthesis of chalcone derivatives were successfully conducted using phenyl acetylenes and benzaldehydes in presence of 1,2-dichloroethane. In the beginning, the solution mixture was flowed continuously by a pump through the reaction vessel charged with Amberlyst-15 as a solid acid catalyst, which was inserted in a reactor equipped with microwave generator (50 W) in a defined time. Finally, solution of the crude product was collected from the outlet tube, and then purified chromatographically. The electron-poor or electron-rich substrates are tolerable in this reaction condition and the corresponding products are obtained in good yield [13].

Attractive synthetic protocols have also been developed to pursue high reaction yield and to minimize the side reaction. By Suzuki reaction Chalcones could be synthesized employing cynnamoyl-chloride and phenyl boronic acids as reagents in presence of Pd catalyst under basic reaction condition(**Scheme 6**) [14].

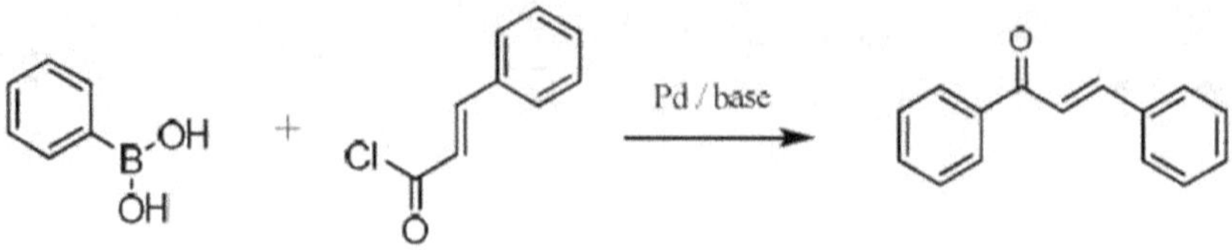

Scheme 6: Synthesis of Chalcone derivatives using Suzuki reaction conditions

Carbonylative Heck coupling reaction employing Pd as catalyst is another protocol to produce chalcone by the reaction between aryl halide and styrene in the presence of carbon monoxide(Scheme 7) [15].

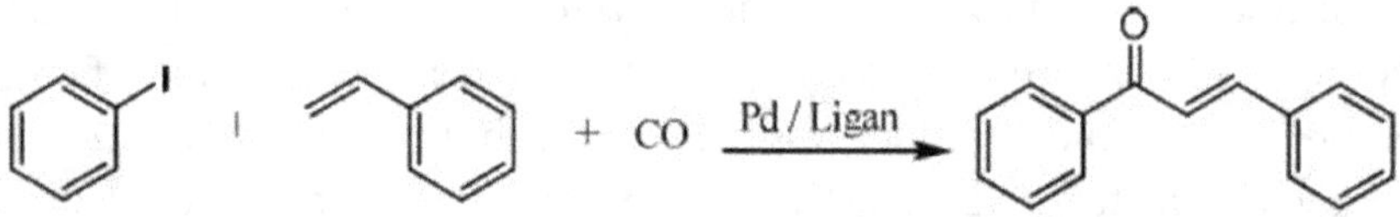

Scheme 7: Synthesis of Chalcone derivatives using Heck coupling reaction conditions

The Wittig reaction is one more straightforward method to create alkene compounds. Chalcone is a reasonable alkene template for the Wittig reaction strategy **(Scheme 8)**. Initially triphenylbenzoylmethylene phosphorane was treated with benzaldehyde for 3 days of reflux in benzene or 30 h in THF with a fair yield of 70%[16,17]. Further development has indicated by that the synthesis of various chalcones using eight aromatic aldehydes can be carried out in 5–6 min using microwave irradiation methods with good yields (>80%)[18].

Scheme 8: Synthesis of Chalcone derivatives using Wittg reaction conditions

In general the Friedel-Crafts acylation is an organic reaction employed to convert an aryl compound and an acyl halide or anhydride to an aryl ketone in presence of a Lewis acid catalyst . In this reaction Lewis acid abstracts the halide from the acyl halide resulting in an electrophilic acylium cation and a tetrasubstituted aluminum anion. In the next step, the aromatic compound attacks the acylium ion *via* an electrophilic aromatic substitution resulting in a cationic product with loss of aromaticity. Finally, deprotonation with the aluminum anion produces a aryl ketone and regeneration of the Lewis acid catalyst[19]. Friedel−Crafts acylation of an aromatic ether and cinnamoyl chloride in the presence of a strong Lewis acid catalyst, such as aluminum trichloride, results in chalcones. This method was reported by Shotter et al. in 1978, with four chalcones made in fair yields[20].

References

1. G Yoon; BY Kang; SH Cheon, Arch. Pharm. Res., 2007, 30(3), 313.

2. H.D Durst; GW Gokel, Experimental Organic Chemistry., 2nd Edition, McGraw-Hill Publishing Company, New York, 1987, 428.

3. S Sebti; A Solhi; R Tahir; S Boulaajaj; JA Mayoral; JM Fraile; A Kossir; H Oumimoun, Tetrahedron Lett., 2001, 42, 7953.

4. K Watanabe; AImazawa, Bull. Chem. Soc. Jpn., 1982, 55, 3208.

5. M.S Cheng; R.S Li; G Kenyon, Chin ChemLett., 2000, 11(10), 851.

6. P Salehi; MM Khodaei; MA Zolfigol; A Keyvan, MonatsheftefuerChemie., 2002, 133, 1291.

7. F Fringuelli; F Pizzo; C Vittoriani; L Vaccacio, Chem. Commun., 2004, 130, 2756.

8. G Thinurayanan; G Vanangamudi, E-Journal of Chemistry.,2007, 4(1), 90.

9. Z.N Siddiqui; T.N.M. Musthafa, Tetrahedron Lett.,2011, 52, 4008.

10. M. Zeng; L Wang; J Shao; Q Zhong, Synth Commun.,1997, 27(2), 351.

11. D. Kakati; JC Sarma, Chemistry Central Journal., 2011, 5, 8.

12. M.R. Jayapal; KS Prasad; NY Sreedhar, J. Chem. Pharm. Res., 2010, 2(3), 127.

13. M. Rueping; T. Bootwicha; H. Baars; E. Sugiono, Beilstein. J. Org. Chem., 2011, 7, 1680.

14. S. Eddarir; N. Cotelle; Y. Bakkour; C. Rolando, Tetrahedron Lett.,2003, 44, 5359.

15. L.W Xu; L Li; CG Xia; PQ Zhao, Helv. Chem. Acta., 2004, 87, 3080.

16. Bestmann, H. J.; Arnason, B. Reaktionen mit Phosphinalkylenen, II. C-Acylierung von Phosphin-alkylenen. Ein neuer Weg zur Synthese von Ketonen. Chem. Ber. 1962, 95, 1513.

17. F.Ramirez,; S.Dershowitz, Phosphinemethylenes.1 II. Triphenylphosphineacylmethylenes. J. Org. Chem. 1957, 22, 41.

18. C.Xu,; G.Chen,; X.Huang, Chalcones by the wittig reaction of a stable ylide with aldehydes under microwave irradiation. Org. Prep. Proced. Int. 1995, 27, 559.

19. E.Ador,; J.Crafts, *Ber. Dtsch. Chem. Ges.* **1877**, *10*, 2173.

20. R. G.Shotter,; K. M.Johnston,; J. F. Jones, Reactions of unsaturated acid halides IV1: Competitive friedel-crafts acylations and alkylations of monohalogenobenzenes by the bifunctional cinnamoyl chloride. Tetrahedron 1978, 34, 741.

CHAPTER FOUR

Reactivity of Chalcones

"If you want to have good ideas, you must have many ideas."

Linus Pauling

Chalcone represent the central core of biologically active hetrocyclic compounds.They represent good synthons for a variety of novel hetrocycles of high pharamaceutical profile and therapeutic potential. Chalcone (1,3-diphenyl-2-propen-1-one) is a phenolic compound which is abundant in natural plants(**Fig.1 and Fig.2**).They are reactive towards a number of reagents. These chalcones have been found to be useful for the syntheses of variety of Heterocyclic compounds. Chalcones are structural analogues of benzalacetophenone (BAP, 1,3-diphenyl-2-propen-1-one). Hydroxylated and methoxylated derivatives of the parent molecule are secondary plant constituents (flavonoids). These chalcones possess a wide variety of cytoprotective and modulatory functions, which may have therapeutic potential for multiple diseases. Physicochemical properties of Chalcones seem to define the extent of their biological activity. Hence understanding their chemical reactivity becomes important. Some of the important reactions are described as below.

4.1.Reaction of α:β-dibromo Chalcones with hydroxylamine hydrochloride

The alcoholic solution of α-β dibromochalcones when refluxed with molar proportion of hydroxylamine hydrochloride and aqueous potassium hydroxide, followed by acidification, yield that 2-isoxazole derivatives.

Scheme 1: Reaction of α:β-dibromo Chalcones with hydroxylamine hydrochloride

4.2.Reaction of α:β-dibromo chalcones with benzene-1,2-diamine

Reaction of α-β dibromoChalcones with benzene-1,2-diamine in methanol in presence of acid catalyst afforded quinoxaline derivatives.

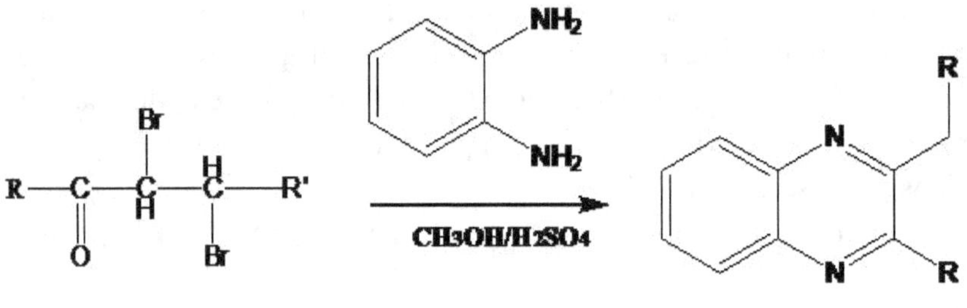

Scheme 2: Reaction of α:β-dibromo Chalcones with hydroxylamine hydrochloride

Fig .1: Garcinia indica Choisy (Natural Source of Chalcones)

Fig. 2 : Bacopa monnieri (Natural Source of Chalcones)

4.3. Reaction of Chalcones with bromine

The Chalcone adds a molecule of bromine and under usual conditions α,β- dibromo Chalcone is obtained.

Scheme 3: Reaction of Chalcones with bromine

Dibromide of simplest benzylidene acetophenone is prepared by Claisen and Clasparede [1]. Action of bromine on Chalcones derived from some o-hydroxyacetophenone is studied by Vanderwalla and Jadhav. One molecule of bromine is found to act at the ethylenic bond. Dibromides are prepared using acidic medium [2]. Initially bromine enters the double bond very easily and if the reaction is continued, bromine enters the nucleus also[3]. Further, it is seen that styryl nucleus in Chalcones is more reactive than the aryloxy part.

4.4. Replacement of oxygen by sulphur in 2-isoxazoline derivatives

Reactions of P_2S_5 in pyridine are the replacement of ring oxygen by sulfur atom. Treatment of 2-isoxazoline with phosphorous pentasulfide in pyridine yielded 2-isothiazoline derivatives.

4.5. Reaction of hydrazine hydrate with Chalcones

On treating chalcone with hydrazine in presence of ethanol results in pyrazole derivatives

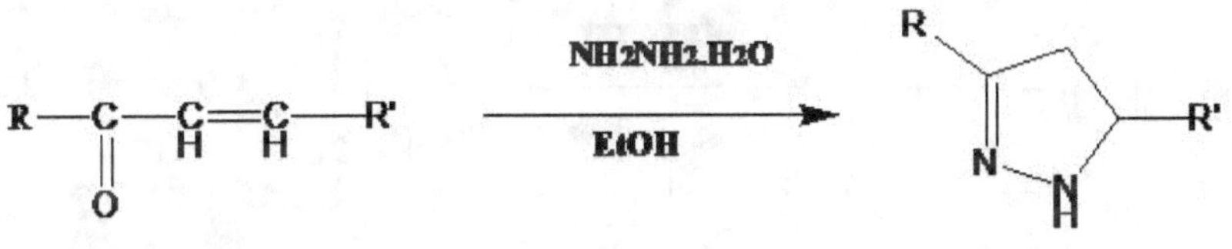

Scheme 4: Reaction of hydrazine hydrate with Chalcones

4.6. Reaction of Chalcones with Urea

Scheme 5: Reaction of Chalcones with Urea

Pyrimidinone derivatives [4] are prepared by heating Chalcone derivatives with urea in ethanolic hydrochloric acid.

4.7. Reaction of Chalcones with 2-aminothiophenol

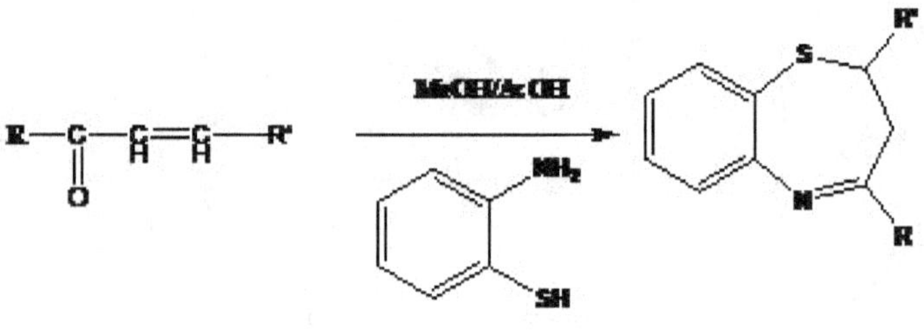

Scheme 6: Synthesis of 1, 5-benzothiazepine derivatives.

Chalcones on reaction with 2-Aminothiophenol in the presence of glacial acetic acid and methanol gave propiophenones which immediately undergo cyclization gave 1, 5-benzothiazepine derivatives.

4.8. Reaction of Thiourea with Chalcones

Scheme 7: Synthesis of Pyrimidine-2-thione derivatives

On heating benzalacetophenone derivatives with thiourea in ethanolic hydrochloric acid and resulting mixture is treated with acetylchloride resulting in the acetyl derivatives of pyrimidine- 2- thiones.

4.9. Reaction of Chalcones with p-toluidine

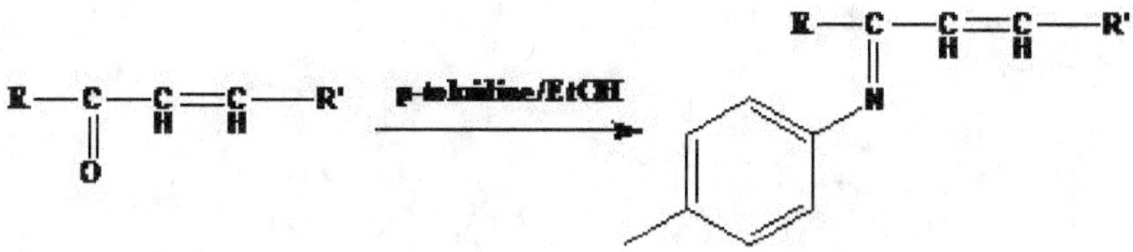

Scheme 8: Synthesis Reaction of Chalcones with p-toluidine

Chalcones reacts with p-toluidine in absolute alcohol to give corresponding Schiff bases.

4.10. Reaction of chalcones with monoethanolamine

Scheme 9: Synthesis 1,4-oxazapine derivatives derivatives

Chalcones reacts with monoethanolamine in absolute alcohol to give corresponding 1,4-oxazapine derivatives [5].

4.11. Reaction of Chalcones with guanidine nitrate

Treating 2-arythydrazone-1-phenylaminobutane-1-3-diones with guanidine nitrate results in 2-aminopyrimidine derivatives[6]. Chalconoids when reacted with guanidine nitrate in the presence of aqueous sodium hydroxide (40%) in ethanol gave 2-aminopyrimidine derivatives, which on treatment with sodium nitrite in presence of glacial acetic acid resulted in the corresponding 2-pyrimidinone derivatives. Additionally the reaction of 2-amino, pyrimidine derivatives with acetic anhydride in acetic acid gave the corresponding diacetyl derivatives [7].

References

1. Arito et al.; *Japan p.,* 1956, 294; *Chem. Abstr.,* **51,** (1957),4054.

2. Shyama Sundar; *Proc. Indian Acad. Sci.,* **59A,** (1964),241 .

3. Arita et al.; Japan 294(56) Jan. 20, US 2, 769, 786 Nov. 6, 1956 See Britt 740, 886, (C.A).50, 10445e).

4. D. H. Marian, P. B. Russel and A. R. Todd;*J. Chem. Soc.*, **1419** (1947).

5. A.C. Grosscurt, H. R. Van and K. Wellinga; *J. Agric. Food Chem.*, **27(2)**,(1979),406 .

6. E. T. Ogansyna et al.; *Khim. Farm. Zh.*, **25(8)**, 18 (1991); *Chem. Abstr.*, **115,** 247497n(1991).

7. Kamei, Hideo, Koide, Tatsurou, Hashimoto Yoko, Kojima et al.;*Cancer Biother Radio Pharm.*, **12(1)**, (1997), 51-54 .

CHAPTER FIVE

Medicinal Applications of Chalcones

"Science knows no country, because knowledge belongs to humanity, and is the torch which illuminates the world."

– Louis Pasteur

The trouble of cancer is increasing across the humankind and thus it is the leading cause of deaths in even in developed countries and second leading cause of deaths in developing countries [1]. Cancer is regarded as to be one of the most inflexible diseases because of the inherent characteristics of cancer cells to proliferate wildly, avoid apoptosis, invade and metastasize [2]. Even though with the advances in chemotherapy, there are no sufficient clinically valuable cytotoxic agents that selectively target cancer cells.

Generally, chemotherapeutic agents have anticancer activity, thanks to their capacity to elicitapoptosis [3]. The physiologically determined cell death, apoptosis, is necessary to maintain tissue homeostasis. While it provides a mechanism of autodigestion for cells that are not functioning properly, the screening of anticancer agents for chemotherapy is deliberated to identify agents that selectively kill tumor cells. Numerous natural as well as synthetic agents have demonstrated to elicit apoptosis in cancer cells [4]. Synthetic derivatives are often established to be more active than parent compounds [5].

Chalconoid, considered as the precursors of flavonoids and isoflavonoids are extensively found in edible plants[6,7]. They consist of open-chain flavonoids in which the two aromatic rings are joined by a three-carbon α,β-unsaturated carbonyl system. Among the flavonoids, chalcones are an remarkable target class of compounds which are comprehensively investigated owing to their broad spectrum of biological activities *viz.*, anti-invasive , anti-inflammatory, antibacterial , antitumour properties. Chalconoid are considered as promising anticancer agents against most human cancers. They are competent of inducing apoptosis and have the ability to uncouple mitochondrial respiration thereby collapsing mitochondrial membrane potential [8]. Generally, a number of clinically useful anticancer drugs have genotoxic effects due to their interaction with the amino groups of nucleic acids, chalcones may be devoid of these important side effects [9].

Nitrogen containing heterocyclic derivatives synthesized from chalcones have exhibited antiinflammatory,antioxidant, antitubercular, antibacterial activities.

Chalcones are important constituents of many natural products(**Fig.1 and Fig.2**). They are abundant in edible plants where they are considered to be the precursors of flavonoids and isoflavonoids. Growing interest in the pharmacological potential of chalcones is attributed due to its screening for a wide range of pharmacological activities such as antitumor, antibacterial antifungal antioxidant and anti-inflammatory properties[10,11]. All through the ages mankind is dependent on nature, particularly on plants as source of carbohydrates, proteins and fats for food and shelter. Amid the presence of a wide variety of secondary metabolites, plants have created the basis of the traditional medicine systems that have been in existence for thousands of years in many countries. The flavonoids and allied phenolic and poly phenolic compounds, as well as tannins and derived poly-phenols and their various derivatives form one major group of phytochemicals. In numerous plants flavonoids protect them against their pathogenic bacteria and fungi. The Homo sapience is the main beneficiary of the dietary flavonoids knowing or unknowingly utilizes them for avoidance of diseases or cure. Their antioxidant properties,cytostatic effects in tumorigenesis and capability to inhibit a broad spectrum of enzymes have led researchers to regard these compounds as potential cardio protective and anticarcinogens agents[12,13].

Fig .1: Pongamia pinnata (Natural Source of Chalcones)

Fig. 2 : Primula macrophylla (Natural Source of Chalcones)

During the current century, Chalcone,the aromatic ketone, have found lot of applications. Several Chalcones exhibit therapeutic properties e.g. anticular activity, hypotensive activity etc. Antibiotic activity [14] have shown by some Chalcones owing to presence of enone operate. Generally, antiseptic property gets enhanced with the introduction of a substituent sort of a nitro or bromo cluster at the β -position or a bromo or hydroxyl at the β-position. They possess biological properties and they prove prejudicious to the expansion of microbes [15] tubercle bacilli protozoal infection parasites viscus worms etc. These aromatic ketone additionally inhibit growth of many enzymes and fungi [16].

Therapeutic Interest

Chalcones, also known as chalconoid, have been found to possess wide range of therapeutic Activities [17] *viz.,*

a. Antiviral
b. Antitubercular
c. Antiulcer,
d. Anthelmintics
e. Antitumor
f. Anticancer
g. Anti HIV
h. Fungicidal
i. Herbicidal
j. Insecticidal
k. Bactericidal
l. Cardiovascular
m. Antiallergic
n. Anti-inflammatory
o. Antispasmodic

Chalcones are potential biocides, because some naturally occurring antibiotics and amino chalcones, probably own their biological activity in the presence of α, β-unsaturated carbonyl group(Table 1). Chalcones have been proved to be an important intermediate for the synthesis of many heterocyclic compounds in organic chemistry[18,19].

Table 1: Representative Chalcones and their activities

Entry No.	Name	Structure	Activity
1	Fluorine-substituted synthetic chalcone	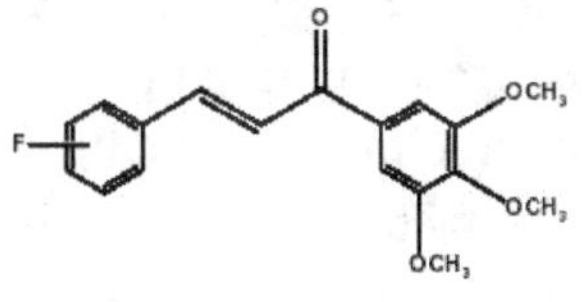	Antitubercular agents
2	Thiophenyl flavonoids	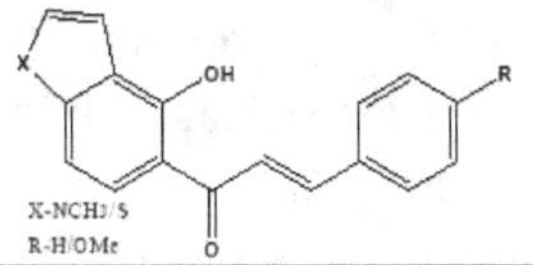	Antifungal and antibacterial activity
3	Heteroaryl substituted chalcones	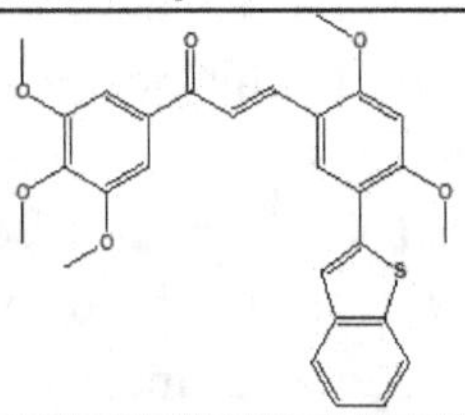	Inhibitors of TNF-alpha-induced VCAM-1 expression
4	Myrigalone	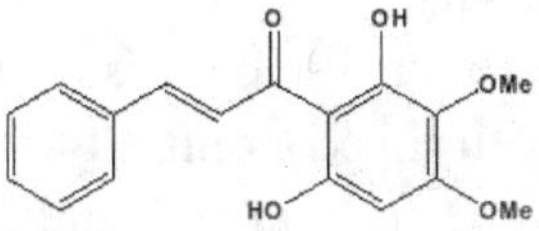	Antiviral activity
5	Penta-oxygenated chalcone	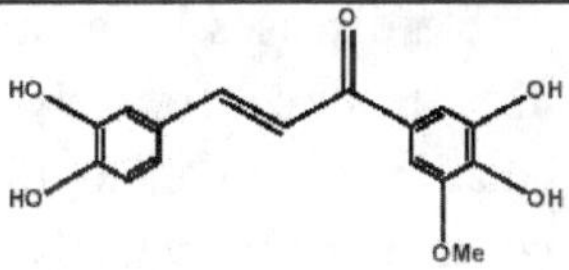	Potent DPPH radical activity
6	β-hydroxy chalcone	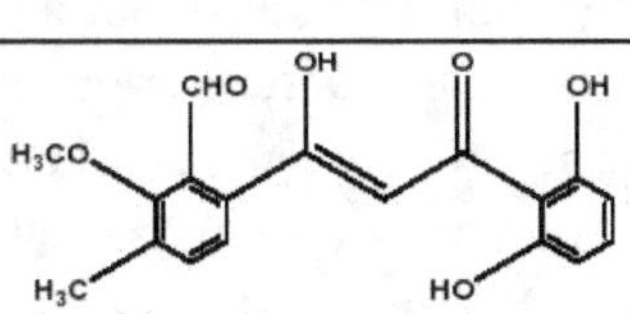	Anti-HIV activity

5.1 Antioxidant

Free radicals have been concerned in the etiology of several human diseases, as well as ageing. Numerous studies indicate that mitochondrial reactive oxygen species (ROS) production and oxidative damage to mitochondrial DNA results in ageing. The most common form of neurodegenerative disease associated with dementia in elderly people is Alzheimer's disease (AD) [20]. Evidence suggests that AD pathogenesis involves an imbalance between free radical formation and destruction. This notion initially resulted from the free radical hypothesis of aging, with age-related accumulation of free radicals resulting in damaged cell components. That age is a prime threat factor in AD provides support for this assumption.

5.2. Antimicrobial Activity

Chalconoids (1, 3-diphenyl-propene-1-one) belonging to the flavonoid family, are natural and synthetic products that have attracted attention due to their extensive range of biological activities as antibacterial anti-tumor, anti-inflammatory and antioxidant agents, *etc*. Even though studies on the bioavailability of heterocyclic Chalcones from natural sources are limited, they exhibit a wide range of biological activities, especially antibacterial, and antifungal activities [21]. In an endeavor to expand the biological activities of conventional Chalcones, a series of heterocyclic chalcone analogues, in which an electron rich nitrogen or oxygen as well as thiophene heterocycle replacing the benzene ring, were reported [22-26].

5.3. Anticancer Activity

The burden of cancer is increasing across the World and thus it is the leading cause of deaths in economically developed countries and second leading cause of deaths in developing countries Cancer is considered to be one of the most intractable diseases because of the innate characteristics of cancer cells to proliferate uncontrollably, avoid apoptosis, invade and metastasize. Despite the advances in chemotherapy, there are no sufficient clinically useful cytotoxic agents that selectively targets cancer cells.

Amid the currently identified antitumor agents, chalcones represent an important class of molecules. Deregulation of apoptosis or programmed cell death, in multicellular organisms is a key contributor to the survival of tumour cells. The practice of apoptosis can be divided into two parts, sensors and effectors. The sensors (extrinsic pathway) are accountable for monitoring the extracellular and intracellular environment for conditions that influence whether a cell should live or die. These signals regulate the second class of components (intrinsic pathway or mitochondrialapoptosis pathway), which induces apoptotic death. Chalcones have been found to act through the intrinsic as well as extrinsic apoptosis pathway to prevent tumour progression.Traditions from different geographical regions of the world and different time periods have documented the extensive use of liquorice for the cure of different human ailments including as an anti-ulcer agent. Modern studies have identified different chalcones and flavonoids as the active ingredients for their activity. Chalcones like isoliquiretigenin, licochalcone A and licochalcone E have been isolated from liquorice and reported to be effective against a series of human cancer cell lines[27,28].

Most of the chemotherapeutic agent has anticancer activity thanks to their capacity to elicit apoptosis. The physiologically determined cell death, apoptosis, is necessary to maintain tissue homeostasis; where homeostasis refers to the balance between cell proliferation and cellular loss [29]. Since it provides a mechanism of auto digestion for cells that are not functioning properly, the screening of anticancer agents for chemotherapy is designed to identify agents that selectively kill tumor cells [30].

References

1. Jemal, A.; Bray, F.; Center, M.M.; Ferlay, J.; Ward, E.; Forman, D. Global cancer statistics. CA Cancer J. Clin.2011, 61, 69.

2. Hiss, D.C.; Gabriels, G.A. Implications of endoplasmic reticulum stress, the unfolded protein response and apoptosis for molecular cancer therapy. Part I: targeting p53, Mdm2, GADD153/CHOP, GRP78/BiP and heat shock proteins. Expert Opin.Drug Discov.2009, 4, 799.

3. Johnstone, R.W.; Ruefli, A.A.; Lowe, S.W. Apoptosis-A Link between Cancer Genetics and Chemotherapy. Cell 2002, 108, 153.

4. Gordaliza, M. Natural products as leads to anticancer drugs. Clin. Trans. Oncol. 2007, 9, 767.

5. Anand, P.; Kunnumakkara, A.B.; Newman, R.A.; Aggarwal, B.B. Bioavailability of curcumin: problems and promises. Mol. Pharm. 2007, 4, 807.

6.Aluru Rammohan,Julakanti Satyanarayana Reddy,Gundala Sravya,Chittluri Nara; · Grigory V. Zyryanov, Chalcone synthesis, properties and medicinal applications: A review, Environmental Chemistry Letters (2020) 18:433.

7.Chunlin Zhuang,Wen Zhang,Chunuguan Sheng,Wannia Zhang,Chengguo Xing ,Zhenyuan Miao, Chalcne: A Privileged Structure in Medicinal Chemistry, Chem Rev.(2017) 117(12): 7762

8. Hijova, E. Bioavailability of chalcones. BratislLekListy2006, 107, 80.

9. Zhang, H.J.; Qian, Y.; Zhu, D.D.; Yang, X.G.; Zhu, H.L. Synthesis, molecular modeling and biological evaluation of chalconethiosemicarbazide derivatives as novel anticancer agents. Eur. J. Med. Chem. 2011, 46, 4702.

10. Alcaraz, L.E.; Blanco, S.E.; Puig, O.N.; Tomas, F.; Ferretti, F.H. Antibacterial activity of flavonoids against methicillin-resistant Staphylococcusaureusstrains. J. Theor. Biol. 2000, 205, 231.

11. Alcaraz, L.E.; Blanco, S.E.; Puig, O.N.; Tomas, F.; Ferretti, F.H. Antibacterial activity of flavonoids against methicillin-resistant Staphylococcus aureusstrains. J. Theor. Biol. 2000, 205, 231.

12. Rao, S. R.; Ravishankar, G. A. Biotechnol. Adv. 2002,20, 101.

13. Cowan, M. M. Clin. Microbiol.Rev .1999,12, 564.

14.Tashio Pharmaceutical Co Ltd.; 271 Japan, Kokai Tokkyo Koho Jp., 51, 12, 094 (Cl A 61 K 31/215); Chem. Abstr., 101,54722j (1984).

15 M. R. Bell; US Appl., 637, 931 (1984); Chem. Abstr., 113, 211828t (1990).

16 Guo Zongru, Han Rui; CN 1, 13, 909, Chem. Abstr., 125, 103768 (1996).

17.N. Lall, A. A. Hussein and J. J. M. Meyer; Fitoterapia, 77(3), 230-232 (2006).

18.Sarot Cheenpracha, Chatehanok Karalai, Supinya Tewtrakul; Bioorganic & Medicinal Chemistry, 14(6), 1710-1714 (2006).

19.Y. Inamori et al.; Chem. Pharm. Bull., 39(6), 1604 (1991); Chem. Abstr., 115, 105547c (1991).

20.E. Marmo, A. P. Caputi and S. Cataldi; Farmaco Ed. Prat., 28(3), 132 (1973); Chem. Abstr.,79, 13501v (1973).

21.S. R. Modi and H. B. Naik; Orient J. Chem., 10(1), 85-6 (1994); Chem. Abstr., 122, 81186c (1995) 272

22.L. Nelson George; U.S. US 4,338,499 (Cl. 568-343; CO7C49/597), 06 Jul (1982), Appl. 250, 366, 02 Apr (1981) 7 .

23.P.Prem.Yadav, P. K.Prasoon Gupta, Shukla and Rakesh Mavrya; Bioorganic & Medicinal Chemistry, 13(5) (2005) 1497 .

24.C. Q.Meng and X. S.Zheng; Bioorg Med. Chem. Lett., 14(6), 1513-1517 (2004).

25.a) J. R.Cole, S. J.Torrance, R. H.Weiedgopf, S. K.Arora and R. B.Bates;J. Org. Chem., 41,1852 (1976). b) V. K. Ahluwalia, Neelu Kaila and Shashi Bala; Indian J. Chem., 25B, (1986)663 .

26. O.Nerya, R.Musa, S. Khatib, S.Tamir, J. Vaya; Photochemistry., 65(10) (2004) 1389 .

27.N.S. Rao, C. Kistareddy, B. Balram, B. Ram, Der PharmaChemica, 4(6) (2012) 2408.

28.C.M. Bhalgat, M.I. Ali, B. Ramesh, G. Ramu, Ara J Chem., 2011 1-8.

29.A. K. Pedersen and G. A. Fitz Gerald; J. Pharm. Sci., **74(2)**, 188 (1985).

30.S.Parmar Virinder, C. Jain Subhash et al.; Indian J. Chem., Sect. B., Org. Chem. Incl Med. Chem., **37B (7)**, (1998) 628 .

CHAPTER SIX

Conclusion

In this book on Recent Advances in Chalcones Chemistry, the nature, structure, classification, acitivities and applications of Chalcones have been thoroughly discussed in the preceeding five chapters. The authors have made an attempt to bring in the latest developments in Chalcones Chemistry by discussing the impacts of structural features, the biological activities, their role to treat diseases including cancer. To sum up, the significant advances in Chalcones Chemistry have been enlisted here.

- Chalcones (1,3-diaryl-2-propen-1-ones) constitute an important class of natural products belonging to the flavonoid family, which possess a wide spectrum of biological activities, including antibacterial, antifungal, anti-inflammatory, antitumor, insect anti-feedant and antimutagenic .
- Chalcones are classified into two types namelyNatural chalcones and Synthetic Chalcones based on the source of generation. The anti-inflammatory effects of chalcones in vertebrates have all been reported in vitro. Thus, it is essential to establish an effective animal model to study in vivo the anti-inflammatory effects of chalcones.
- Microwave irradiation induced reaction in the chalcones synthesis is an alternative procedure to synthesize chalcones. This reaction method can shorten the reaction time and simplify the purification procedure. An attractive single step synthesis protocol of chalcone was reported, in which chalcones were synthesized using molecular iodine impregnated over neutral alumina as catalyst, and employing microwave irradiation as source of energy without any solvent.
- More exotic synthetic protocols have also been developed to pursue high reaction yield and to minimize the side reaction. Chalcone could be synthesized using Suzuki reaction, employing cynnamoyl-chloride and phenyl boronic acids as reagents and Pd as catalyst in base reaction

condition.
- Chalcones like isoliquiretigenin, licochalcone A and licochalcone E have been isolated from liquorice and reported to be effective against a series of human cancer cell lines.
- In an effort to diversify the biological activities of conventional Chalcones, a series of heterocyclic chalcone analogues in which an electron rich nitrogen or oxygen as well as thiophene heterocycle replaces the benzene ring have been synthesized.

- Some dihydrochalcones are well known for their sweetening property, and appear to be non-nutritive sweeteners. A dihydrochalcone Uvaretin from *Uvaria acuminata* has shown antitumor activity in lymphocytic leukemia test.